Fleaona
The Vegetarian Cat

To the Falls family,
I hope you enjoy the
story. Love,
♡ RBradford

Written by: Rebekah Bradford

Illustrated by: Candice Landsberg

Words to watch for:

baffle
bizarre
finicky
habit
indigestion
jubilant
opt
pluot
ponder
rant
saunter
scowl
variety
vegetarian

Dedicated to our children:
RB: Liam, Kellen, and Quinn
CL: Bettie and Siouxsie Q.

On the porch of a tiny blue house in the city
lived a fluffy gray cat whose coat was quite pretty.
Her name was Fleaona, though some called her Flea,
and her habits of eating were
something to see.

Whenever before her was placed meat or fish,
Fleaona would scowl and abandon her dish.
She did not desire cat food from a can,
nor would she consider roast turkey or ham.

You see, this cat had a curious rant.
When asked to eat lunch, she would object,

The Neighborhood cats found Fleaona bizarre.
They laughed at her finicky eating.
They saw her admiring plants from afar, and carefully,
with her paws, weeding.

"She pays such attention to
bushes and trees
and couldn't care less about
spiders or bees.
What's wrong with this
creature,
this mystery cat?"

They pondered while gazing at Flea
where she sat..

"She looks like we do, but acts similar never.
Is this cat confused, or unusually clever?"
One thing was for sure-
they planned to learn more.
Was there a new diet that they should explore?

For hours, Fleaona gave free entertainment
to Fritz and Monroe, who could offer no payment.
So baffled they were by their plant-loving neighbor,
they sauntered right over to ask for a favor.

"May we come and play?" asked the calico, Fritz.
"My friend here, Monroe, and I, like to do tricks.
If we show them to you,
will you teach us a few
very interesting facts about sticks?"

"About sticks?" laughed Fleaona.
"You mean all of these?"
She motioned around to the flowers and trees,
"Why, these are not sticks, they are blooming and growing,
not unlike the grass, which requires weekly mowing.
Since you've much to learn, I guess I'll do the showing."

Fritz and Monroe, so excited to know
all the marvelous things she was doing,
listened to every word Flea said, without so much
as mewing.

And they did some gymnastics- their end of the deal,
then invited Fleaona to share their next meal.

"I'm not certain," she said,
"though I like the suggestion.
If I eat what you like, I'll get indigestion!
Perhaps, if you wish to taste something delish,
you'll try some of these vegetables next to your fish!"
Fritz and Monroe agreed,
they did probably need some variety in their diet.
So they asked for a sampling of things she had grown.
and they promised to happily try it.

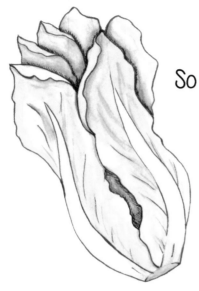

So Fleaona brought portions of lettuce

and spinach,

and blueberries,

which were most speedily finished.

Dessert was oranges,

Melon and clover.

They all ate so much, they nearly fell over!

New fanatics were born in Monroe and in Fritz.
They were such produce fans,
they threw jubilant fits
and ate peaches and pluots right down to the pits.

"Fleaona, we thank you for sharing these flavors-
the fruits and the vegetables of your hard labor.
We know you must water and weed everday.
So with our four paws, we are cheering HOORAY!"

And from that day on,
Flea was never alone.
She had two eager friends to call her very own.
Though they'd once thought her strange, they had realized that
she was one super-cool vegetarian cat!

And while Fritz and Monroe didn't stop eating meat,
they did opt for more fruit, which was juicy and sweet.
And together for dinner they'd gather and eat,

with vegetables nestled in colorful heaps:

squash,
cauliflower,
zucchini,
green beans,
yams,
bell peppers,
tomatoes

Corn, onions, garlic, and green little peas,

plus carrots, broccoli and potatoes.

The cat friends had all learned to keep their minds open to new things
to do and to eat,
and mostly to new friends, who though sometimes different, were
always a wonderful treat!

The End,
Friends!

Glossary:
(what all those wacky new words mean)

baffle: (baf-uh-l) verb- to confuse (someone) completely

bizarre: (bih-zahr) adjective- very unusual or strange

finicky: (fin-i-kee) adjective- very hard to please

habit: (hab-it) noun- something that a person does often in a regular and repeated way

indigestion: (in-di-jes-chuhn) noun- an unpleasant feeling in the stomach caused by difficulty in digesting food

jubilant: (joo-buh-luhnt) adjective- having or expressing great joy

opt: (opt) verb- to choose one thing instead of another

pluot: (ploo-ot) noun- a fruit that is a hybrid, or mix, of plum and apricot

ponder: (pon-der) verb- to think about or consider (something) carefully

rant: (rant) verb- to talk loudly in a wild or urgent manner.

saunter: (sawn-ter) verb- to walk along in a slow and relaxed manner; stroll

scowl: (skoul) verb- to look at someone or something in a way that shows anger or disapproval

variety: (vuh-rahy-i-tee) noun- a number or collection of different things

vegetarian: (vej-i-tair-ee-uhn) noun- a person who does not eat meat